Even though we are not born coaches, it is within our role as managers to have career and professional development discussions with our employees. Career ambitions are important to all-around well-being and a sense of satisfaction in our work, although many of us feel ill-equipped for such discussions with employees. Still, four trends that will continue for the next several years make it crucial for managers to learn now how to create a culture of development.

1. Unemployment continues to decrease. According to the U.S. Bureau of Labor Statistics, unemployment reached a low of 5.3 percent as of July 2015. We are beyond the recession, resulting in more career opportunities for employees who are not hesitant about moving on. In particular, high-potential employees are most at risk for seeking (and being sought for) more promising options outside their companies. An added challenge to retention is the easy accessibility of job listings and online and mobile application processes.

2. Workplace cultures are becoming more multigenerational. Boomers and Gen Xers are still prevalent in the workplace; however, Millennials are moving up, and in many cases are assuming leadership roles. According to a 2014 *Forbes* article, at Ernst & Young, 59 percent of managers are Millennials and 18 percent are senior managers, even though many have not been trained to become managers. Additionally, Generation Z (born between 1994 and 2010) is emerging as the next generation preparing to enter the workforce.

3. Technology continues to evolve and change at astonishing speed. Implications for workplace changes include:

- the need to learn new and changing business technologies

- increased ability to work remotely

- easier access to new job opportunities, both within and outside the company

- managers keeping their teams' abilities current, so their performance matches the pace of change.

Additionally, the prevalence of social media exponentially increases everyone's networking capability regardless of cost, location, status, and culture. Likewise, recruiters are also able to network, making it easier to access and entice potential talent in an increasingly competitive market.

4. Power has shifted from employers to employees. More workers are saying no to full-time employment. Some workers have grown frustrated with repeated layoffs and the treatment they receive as job candidates. Technology enables more workers to become free agents, and more virtual opportunities are available that are unhindered by geographical boundaries. By managing several part-time contracts, freelancers can have a flexible schedule and work-life balance, giving them significantly more control over their earnings. Furthermore, the Affordable Care Act has reduced the dependence on health insurance from employers, removing one more reason to work full time for one company.

Keeping these trends in mind, managers need realistic approaches they can use immediately to manage their critical talent resources. Flexibility in worker abilities will help managers handle constantly shifting supply, demand, and demographic variables.

This *TD at Work* is a primer intended for managers, human resources professionals, and others. It is a practical, go-to guide that will explain:

- why career development is important to the organization, employee, and manager

- who is responsible for specific aspects of the employee development process

- how to facilitate the employee development process

- the characteristics of a strong individual development process

- how to lead successful development discussions.

WHY EMPLOYEE DEVELOPMENT?

In a competitive global business landscape, company leaders and employees are wise to adopt continuous, agile learning practices. While employees should manage their careers for ongoing employability, companies should focus on attracting and retaining high-potential, promotable people.

Employee development has an upwardly beneficial impact, from employee to manager to organization. The potential advantages are numerous and dramatic. Best-practice companies, such as Genentech, realize the importance of investing in their employees' development. Genentech has received accolades from the training and development world for initiatives like its CareerLab. A blog post from career development firm Career Systems International further details the notable benefits achieved by the company's dedication to employee development:

- The employee turnover rate is at 6.2 percent, in contrast with the industry average of 11 percent.

- Almost half of the job openings are filled by internal candidates.

- Approximately $20 million in retention cost savings was realized in 2014, when the CareerLab helped find new roles for 76 high-potential employees whose positions were eliminated.

Employee development can be a proactive strategy. Business managers are smart to continually develop their employees even during times of stability, so that they don't wish they had done so when faced with talent shortages.

It is critical to note that employees, not employers, will decide where they will work. Specifically, Millennials, a fast-growing employee

BENEFITS OF EMPLOYEE DEVELOPMENT

Employee development:

- Increases retention.

- Boosts morale.

- Improves person-job match.

- Maintains up-to-date skills for the workforce.

- Provides the resource depth and flexibility needed to swiftly respond to market demands and organizational changes.

- Keeps talent development aligned with organizational strategies.

- Supports and enhances organizational workforce-planning programs.

- Fosters future leaders within the company for business sustainability and stability.

- Increases employee commitment and productivity.

- Attracts high performers to your organization.

- Drives cultural change. For instance, Microsoft implemented a career development system as a strategy to remain competitive. Per a 2007 study, its career model, "platform of common standards," was used to identify, assess, manage, and develop talent as the company shifted its culture.

population, look for employers that will support their development, not just a good salary. A 2015 EdAssist study of Millennials revealed that almost 60 percent "would pick the job with strong potential for professional development over one with regular pay raises." This holds true even for Millennials with high student loan debt; 66 percent said they would trade regular pay increases for a job with strong employee development potential.

EMPLOYEE DEVELOPMENT HAS AN UPWARDLY BENEFICIAL IMPACT, FROM EMPLOYEE TO MANAGER TO ORGANIZATION.

Employee development encompasses three major considerations:

1. abilities and skills—the employee's current specific skills, knowledge, and competencies that are necessary for the ongoing success of the business

2. organizational needs—the needs and expectations of each role in the organizational structure

3. employee interests—career aspirations, the ability to fulfill current and future roles, identified gaps, personality type, and a plan for development.

Figure 1 displays the intersection of these three components. The ideal target for your employees' development, as shown in Figure 2, is at the overlap of employee interests and organizational needs.

The objective is to maintain employee engagement and retention, and to develop individual and organizational capabilities, especially for promising employees with potential to make significant contributions to organizational imperatives. Otherwise employees are free to take their services to competitors. Your acquired and developed talent are a competitive advantage. An international study of organizational effectiveness by Right Management shows that companies providing career development opportunities are

FIGURE 1. ALIGN SKILLS AND INTERESTS WITH ORGANIZATIONAL NEEDS

SOURCE: ATD INTEGRATED TALENT MANAGEMENT CERTIFICATE PROGRAM

FIGURE 2. TARGET AREA FOR SKILL DEVELOPMENT

SOURCE: ATD INTEGRATED TALENT MANAGEMENT CERTIFICATE PROGRAM

six times more likely to engage key talent and four times less likely to lose them. Findings also indicated that only one-third of employees are fully engaged. Of the top 15 engagement drivers, 10 can be tied to career discussions.

WHO IS RESPONSIBLE FOR WHAT?

Managers are responsible for accomplishing results through others, so they must play a vital role in their employees' development. The time spent developing them will pay off in the form of a motivated, skilled, and productive workforce.

Creating a successful individual development plan (IDP) is possible through a partnership between manager and employee. Although managers take an initial proactive role, employees eventually take active ownership of the plan.

Manager Responsibilities

The role of the manager is to initiate and be supportive of employee development, using company resources to do so.

Specifically, managers should:
- Initiate the process.
- Use company-provided frameworks for career planning.
- Explain the IDP process and its purpose.
- Provide an atmosphere of trust and open communication for their employees to discuss their careers and progress.
- Guide the career and progress discussions.
- Ask questions and listen.
- Identify potential career opportunities for employees.
- Identify learning resources and activities.
- Provide constructive feedback.

Employee Responsibilities

Although it is again increasing, in recent years, employee development has waned. And while it's imperative for managers and organizations to facilitate employee development, employees have specific responsibilities.

Specifically, employees should:
- Provide responses to career-related questions.
- Self-reflect to identify career and development goals.
- Evaluate skills and interests openly.
- Draft an IDP with input from their managers.
- Be open to feedback and taking on new challenges.
- Implement and own the plan.
- Assess progress and initiate follow-ups.

An employee's current role is a point on her career continuum, regardless of her employer. The manager supports the employee here and now, at a particular point on her continuum. Overall, the employee's career path combines short-term and long-term goals in the form of annual IDPs. The manager and the company benefit because the employee gains skills and knowledge necessary for the role to be fulfilled. The employee benefits by gaining the opportunities to earn and learn along her path. At some point in time the employee might move into a different role or leave the company, in which case the manager no longer has a responsibility.

FIGURE 3. SAMPLE CAREER TIMELINE

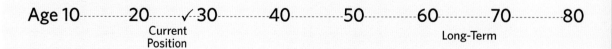

Age 10 ---------- 20 ---------- ✓ 30 ---------- 40 ---------- 50 ---------- 60 ---------- 70 ---------- 80

Current Position

Long-Term

It is worth noting the role of HR in employee development. Generally, HR provides consistent, organization-wide processes, formats, materials, and in some cases technology to facilitate effective IDP planning and implementation. In a word, HR is an enabler: Managers and employees leverage the resources HR gives them to mold unique plans. HR business partners can be valuable guides for managers as well, for pinpointing development activities such as job rotations, international assignments, new positions, and interorganizational assignments.

FACILITATING THE EMPLOYEE DEVELOPMENT PROCESS

Now that we have outlined why an employee development plan is crucial for employee engagement and retention and described the roles of the manager and employee, we'll look at the steps involved in putting the employee development process into practice.

Career and development discussions deserve dedicated space, separate from a performance review meeting. Like a GPS, the IDP process orients you and your employee as to where you are and where to go next. It comprises the key steps as you navigate the map. The base elements of the process consist of the following:

- Articulate career aspirations.

- Assess current interests, skills, knowledge, and abilities.

- Identify strengths and development needs, and decide on goals.

- Create a plan.

- Implement the plan and follow up.

Each element encompasses specific actions that advance discussions and planning along the path. As a manager, you are equipped to facilitate an organized, successful outcome. And by completing these actions, the employee answers the questions:

- Where am I now?

- Where do I want to be?

- How will I get there?

PERFORMANCE REVIEWS VS. DEVELOPMENT PLANS

It is helpful to distinguish between performance reviews and development plans.

Individual performance reviews relate to job responsibilities and goals that ultimately affect business results. The primary view is of the past year. Development, in contrast, is about learning. Employee development is relevant to meeting the needs of the current job, as well as preparing for future opportunities and challenges.

However, there are some similarities. Performance goals are future-focused, for example, and learning supports performance. Learning and performance, in turn, support the business.

Yet even though there is overlap, it's important to keep development discussions separate from performance reviews. This separation promotes safe and open conversations about strengths and development opportunities. Employees won't hesitate because they're afraid of negatively affecting their performance ratings and compensation.

Articulate Career Aspirations— Initial Discussion

The employee development process starts with an eye toward the future. In the long term, where is your employee headed on her career continuum? For the near term, a well-thought-out development plan is a step forward.

The first step is for you to schedule an initial meeting with your employee. Additionally, you must fully prepare for your meeting in advance. This includes taking the time to reflect on the needs of the organization and the employee:

- Consider organizational strategic goals and needs.

- Review the skills, knowledge, and abilities needed for the employee's current position.

- Determine employee development needs with current performance and future potential in mind.

- Decide what questions you will ask.

You should explain the purpose of the meeting to your employee. Is she new to the employee development process? If yes, plan extra time to explain the process, the manager's role, and the employee's role. Think of the first conversation as educational. It is intended to be a positive exchange that sets the stage for subsequent development discussions and creating the plan. It is also a catalyst for exploring and planning how to move toward the employee's aspirations, and learning about the employee's ambitions and motivators.

Here are some tips for conducting the meeting:
- Set and maintain the tone for a positive meeting.
    ◦ Welcome the employee.
    ◦ Ensure privacy—close the door, send phone calls to voicemail, and avoid other distractions.
    ◦ Invite the employee to have a seat.
- Clarify the purpose of the discussion.
    ◦ This is separate from the performance review.
    ◦ It is the first of several meetings to discuss and create the development plan together.

    ◦ Explain that the key difference between performance and development goals is that the latter are focused on learning.

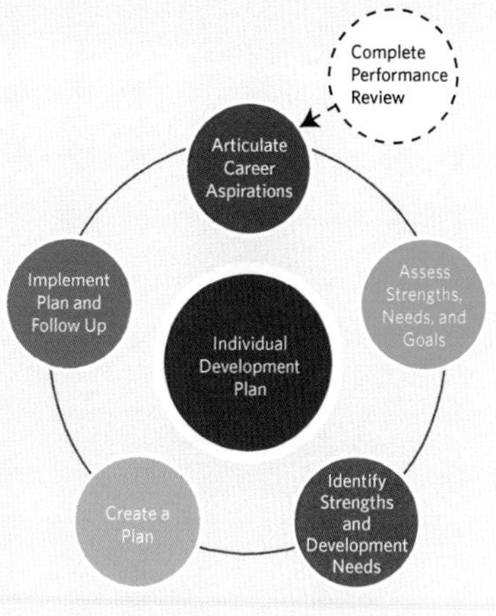

To better ascertain these ambitions and motivators, ask about the employee's interests. This approach can set a positive tone. Ask positive, open-ended questions to spark thinking and possibilities, such as:
- What gives you energy?
- What unique abilities do you offer the world?
- What do you do especially well?
- What do you enjoy doing so much that it doesn't seem like work?
- What accomplishments are you most proud of?

You should also clarify the next steps. Give the employee a list of questions for self-reflection, which will help determine what is important to her and how she sees her career developing. The "Career and Development Discussion Preparation Worksheet" job aid at the end of this issue can serve as an example.

By the end of the first meeting you and your employee should have at least a general idea of the direction of her career path. Some employees will have this well thought out, but this is not always the case. Some employees do not know what they want to do. Others may be close to retirement and not motivated by the idea of a long-term career.

Assess Current Skills, Knowledge, and Abilities

The "articulating career aspirations" and the "assessing current skills, knowledge, and abilities" discussions can occur in the same meeting, or you can have two meetings. This will depend on factors such as whether the employee needs more time to explore career ideas and scheduling availability.

There are numerous ways to assess an employee's current capabilities as sources of input. Depending on your relationship with the employee, you can assess these capabilities by asking open-ended questions as an informal

FIGURE 4. EMPLOYEE DEVELOPMENT PROCESS MAP

SUGGESTED QUESTIONS FOR AN EMPLOYEE DEVELOPMENT MEETING

Initial Discussion

1. What are your career aspirations? What career path or role have you identified?

2. Where would you like to be professionally in two to three years?

3. What have you accomplished that you are most proud of?

4. What do you need to learn to progress toward your goals?

5. What two or three skills or abilities do you want to develop for more success?

6. Are there new tasks or responsibilities that would make even better use of your potential?

7. What do you like most about your current role?

Second Discussion

1. Are there additional challenges that would help you grow and contribute more to the business?

2. Are there certifications or other credentials that would enhance your knowledge and skills for your current role and future career goals?

3. Which additional resources would help you learn new skills and knowledge?

4. What have you considered or learned since our previous discussion?

5. What development activities (projects, committees, other assignments and responsibilities) do you think would help you stretch and fulfill your learning goals?

6. What other activities would you like to engage in that would align with your interests?

7. What are your target dates for completion? Are they realistic?

8. What can I do to help you get started?

9. What can I do to support your ongoing learning?

Follow-Up Checkpoints

1. How are you doing with your plan?

2. What are you learning?

3. Is anything getting in the way that I could address?

4. Is there anything we should change or update on the plan?

approach. The employee can also take a more active role by exploring company job openings to evaluate the gap between her current abilities and that job's requirements.

Additional methods are based on other organization sources, such as development opportunities identified in performance reviews or 360-degree review feedback. If your company has a formal career development system, you can establish next career steps and what the employee needs for the next level.

Be careful not to make direct promises, however, because there is no guarantee. Dynamic organizational changes and approvals outside your control may delay or prevent an actual progression to the next level.

Finally, you can suggest using one of the many widely available career development tools. A gap analysis is useful if the employee has a particular job in mind and wants to compare her current abilities to the job requirements. The June TD at Work bonus issue, "Keeping Your Career on Track," has in-depth instructions on how to conduct a gap analysis.

Identify Strengths and Development Needs

By assessing the gap between current abilities and future aspirations and organizational needs, you and your employee will have determined strengths and areas for development. The areas of development can then be used to create IDP goals. To avoid inundating the employee and perhaps deflating her will to move forward, identify two or three priorities at most for development.

Create a Plan

The tangible output of the employee development process is a robust IDP. Many companies have a preferred form or enterprise software for IDPs. You may also use the job aid at the end of this issue. Regardless of what format you use, the following are typical components of an IDP. Here they are outlined as SLIDE steps:

- **S**et goals.
- **L**ist activities.
- **I**dentify resources.
- **D**etermine success criteria.
- **E**stablish target dates.

Each employee's situation is unique. There are many factors to consider when preparing an IDP, including:

- the depth and breadth of employee responsibilities
- global, virtual, and local teams
- managerial or individual contributors
- specialized skill, knowledge, education, and certification requirements
- the spectrum of entry-level to senior leadership competencies
- ever-changing markets and businesses requiring continuous learning and flexibility
- employee motivation and unique needs for work-life balance
- the gap between where the employee is and future career plans, balanced with organizational needs.

Set the Goals
An IDP should start with at least two specific goals. Some may contain three, depending on the degree of complexity and challenge. For example, your employee may need to learn how to develop and give presentations with confidence in order to be successful at the company and in her career.

List Action Learning Activities
Learning occurs on the job, so it is necessary to look beyond structured courses by seeking a blend of engaging learning activities. Together, identify developmental activities to reach the IDP goals. Possibilities include challenging assignments, job rotations, and leading and participating in project teams or committees. The "Additional Development Options" sidebar provides further ideas for action learning.

ADDITIONAL DEVELOPMENT OPTIONS

Here is a sample list of options for development activities. Some are formal and company-sanctioned, while others are less formal, independent activities.

- Networking
- International assignment
- Provide input on strategic planning
- Volunteer to take on assignments
- Develop others by trusting, delegating, and coaching
- Committee and task force involvement
- Facilitating a learning program
- Give a presentation at a conference
- Job shadowing
- Free online courses at www.edx.org
- Self-paced (books, journals, magazines, self-assessments, YouTube videos, webinars)
- Online learning modules
- Exploratory or informational interviewing
- Assessments
- Review job postings
- Review career ladder at your company
- Find a mentor
- Be a mentor
- Alumni counseling office at your alma mater
- Career Thought Leaders Consortium
- Life coach (International Coach Federation)
- Professional organizations, both inside and outside your area of expertise
- LinkedIn groups
- Management development programs
- Advanced college degree
- Certifications and specialized graduates studies

The action learning activities should be challenging enough to stretch the employee into the learning zone. The comfort zone is where we operate with confidence and competence day to day. The learning, or discomfort, zone is instigated by, for instance, a challenging assignment that requires the use of unfamiliar skill, knowledge, or competence. We often feel awkward or uncomfortable as we learn how to do something new—try writing a few sentences with your opposite hand to get a sense of this. However, with time and repetition we learn to overcome the awkwardness. Avoid providing unrealistic challenges that might cause an employee to experience failure. The intention is to set the employee up for a successful learning experience.

How will the learning goal be accomplished? Help the employee think about steps to take to achieve these development goals. This part of the plan is identifying on-the-job opportunities, such as job shadowing, mentoring, and other learning situations to help people broaden and expand skills in the learning zone. This component of the plan lends itself to thought and creativity. For example, identifying resources that will enable your employee to learn presentation skills is the key outcome of this step. Resources should not be limited to participation in training programs.

Consider ways that she can learn and practice giving presentations. Start with low-risk options for short-term successes, then increase the challenge for more visible situations, such as facilitating training programs or presenting to senior managers.

> ## ONE OF THE BEST WAYS TO DEVELOP EMPLOYEES IS TO DELEGATE MEANINGFUL WORK TO THEM.

One of the best ways to develop employees is to delegate meaningful work to them. There are many benefits to doing this:

- Something that you no longer need to do yourself can become a new learning experience for the developing employee.

- You can provide coaching and mentoring directly.

- It accomplishes work that needs to get done.

- It frees you to focus on more managerial responsibilities.

- It fosters flexibility to have more than one person know how to do a task.

FIGURE 5. EXAMPLE FORCE FIELD ANALYSIS

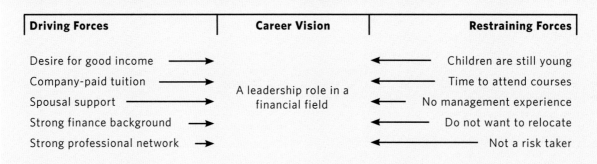

Driving Forces	Career Vision	Restraining Forces
Desire for good income →		← Children are still young
Company-paid tuition →	A leadership role in a financial field	← Time to attend courses
Spousal support →		← No management experience
Strong finance background →		← Do not want to relocate
Strong professional network →		← Not a risk taker

SOURCE: USED WITH PERMISSION FROM THE AUTHOR.

A useful tool in helping an employee identify supporting factors and address barriers toward career progress is Kurt Lewin's Force Field Analysis. Lewin is recognized as the founder of modern social psychology and a pioneer in group dynamics and action research. His frameworks continue to serve as relevant, valued methodologies among agents of change. With this method the employee identifies the driving forces that support her career commitment. Next, she identifies barriers or "restraining" forces and determines what steps to take to remove them. Some factors are personal, and thus must be managed by the employee, while others might be within your control to remove or diminish.

Identify Resources

What resources will be needed for the employee to successfully realize each goal? Resources can take a variety of forms, including people; information; abstract concepts (time, ideas); and materials, for example:

- a mentor who has the skills and knowledge that the employee wants to learn
- books, videos, and articles
- social media, such as Twitter, Yammer, and LinkedIn
- access to senior management
- time to take on new assignments and additional responsibilities
- documents and reports containing relevant information
- funds for tuition, conferences, professional organizations, and certifications.

Determine Success Criteria

How will you know your employee can successfully create and deliver presentations with confidence? Some goals will be easier to measure than others. Some learning activities may be continuous, such as presentation skills. The more we practice, the better we get at it. Regardless, clear criteria for success help you and your employee know if she is progressing and if she has met her objective. In this example success criteria might include:

- self-reporting level of comfort before and after on a 1-5 scale
- completed post-presentation evaluations with rating scales
- enough presentations completed to take on more visible or high-stakes opportunities
- feedback from trusted colleagues in the audience.

Several criteria can be used for each goal.

Establish Target Dates

When will each learning goal be expected to be met? This part is straightforward. Specific begin and end dates should be agreed upon for each goal, such as "January 5–July 31," and not "complete by end of year." If dates are too open-ended it will be hard to gauge progress, and other responsibilities may become barriers.

Implement the Plan and Follow Up

As soon as you and your employee have a final plan in writing, the employee should put it into play. The onus for managing it is on the employee.

How does she keep the plan alive? Once the plan is under way, brief and informal checkpoints can serve as easy ongoing communication. Formal conversations are not necessary, unless both parties prefer otherwise. Checkpoint meetings are opportunities to:

- Find out if your employee is progressing.
- Determine if the plan is having the intended positive impact.
- Adjust the plan, if necessary. Sometimes resources, technology, work environments, or other changes will require adjustments.
- Identify and address any obstacles.

Your ongoing involvement is a show of support that will encourage confidence, motivation, and learning.

CHARACTERISTICS OF A STRONG IDP

The objective of an IDP process is not to complete a form. It is to create a robust, meaningful development plan that has an impact. The following list of characteristics serves as a checklist for determining if you and your employee have a strong IDP.

- **Goals are clear.** Time is well spent in establishing a clear goal of what the employee is aiming to learn. Starting with the goal in mind establishes a destination, like sailing instead of drifting. The remaining components of an IDP are then determined based on this.

- **It follows SMART guidelines (specific, measurable, actionable, realistic, and time-bound).** A plan that is specific and actionable reduces the chances of vagueness and confusion. Having measures and target dates helps determine if the plan is on track once it is in place. A realistic plan is an achievable one. You should gauge how much to push an employee, and if the plan is realistic. In some cases you may not be able to evaluate this until after the plan is in place for a month or two.

- **It stretches the individual into the learning zone.** The activities selected—sometimes referred to as stretch assignments—for development should push employees beyond their current abilities. Some trepidation about going beyond their status quo is normal, so be sure to acknowledge their nervousness and support them.

- **It addresses the learning need.** The point of the plan is for the employee to know and do something differently as identified by the assessment of employee development needs. The plan aims to achieve this goal.

- **It contains a blend of actions.** Adults learn by doing and building on prior experiences. It is also important to note that there are varied learning preferences. A helpful guideline is the well-known 70-20-10 learning model, whereby individuals learn 70 percent through job-related experiences, 20 percent through interactions with others, and 10 percent through formal learning events. A plan that comprises a blend of assignments not only accommodates different learning styles, but can provide built-in reinforcement of learning. For example, an employee can read articles on how to structure a great communication piece. Then the employee should actually write something using the information from the articles. Next, the employee can seek feedback from a trusted colleague to help solidify the learning.

- **It targets changes in behavior.** Behavioral change is the ultimate measure of learning. How would you know if an employee has actually learned to write more effectively? Asking is not evidence. Actually writing and sending a communication that elicits a positive response can clearly be seen. And remember: When interacting with an employee, coaching with questions will reinforce behavior changes; giving directives will not.

> HAVING MEASURES AND TARGET DATES HELPS DETERMINE IF THE PLAN IS ON TRACK ONCE IT IS IN PLACE.

LEADING SUCCESSFUL DEVELOPMENT DISCUSSIONS

Being prepared for any discussion with an employee will increase the probability of productive outcomes for several reasons:

- Being prepared helps you manage your own anxiety and confidence, especially if you do not have much experience with career discussions.

- Being ready with forethought and materials, such as ones from this *TD at Work*, sets you up to conduct your meetings in an organized manner.

- A structured, organized approach saves time.

- It sends a message that you care enough to be prepared for something that's important to the employee.

Approach as a Coach

What is the most powerful question anyone has ever asked you? Invariably, the answer I get to this question is, "When someone asked me, 'Where do you see yourself in five years?'" The most effective approach a manager can use in a career conversation is that of a coach. In this context, coaching is about asking and guiding, not always telling. As Beverly Kaye and Julie Winkle Giulioni wrote in their 2012 T+D article, "Thoughtfully conceived and well-timed questions make things happen. They provoke reflection, insight, constructive discomfort, ideas, and action in others. They keep the focus squarely on the employee and reinforce the shift of development ownership from the manager to the direct report. Finally, effective questions demonstrate that you respect and value the other person."

Make it a rule to practice listening about 80 percent of the time. Asking questions and listening will foster open dialogue and a better understanding of what motivates your employee. Then, by working together you can develop creative options that help you, the employee, and the company reach mutual goals.

> THE MOST EFFECTIVE APPROACH A MANAGER CAN USE IN A CAREER CONVERSATION IS THAT OF A COACH.

Address Challenging Circumstances

While all career discussions should be forward-focused and motivating, some discussions will flow more easily than others. Motivated high-potential employees will likely be enthusiastic and have clear career directions. Some may be unclear, not motivated, or have unrealistic expectations.

Others may be new to the career and development planning process. It is not possible to anticipate all the unique circumstances. Nor should you think that you must have all the answers. However, here are some common challenging scenarios with suggested ways to address them.

Challenge 1: "I've been here for seven years. How come I still don't have the position?"

How to address: Provide the employee with honest feedback. If you are concerned that you might lose the employee, consider that if you don't have the conversation you may still lose him, or worse: He will stay and remain unchanged, de-motivated, unproductive, apathetic, or disgruntled.

Challenge 2: "I don't know what I want to do with my career."

How to address: Suggest the employee use an assessment tool that provides ideas on possible occupations based on values, likes, and strengths. Also, the use of informational interviews can yield insights on positions, fields, industries, and other possible career options. Asking open-ended questions can spark thinking that helps the employee begin to consider possible careers, too.

Challenge 3: Your employee wants to be a vice president someday. However, she has a history of poor communication and an inability to work effectively with others.

How to address: Use open-ended questions to understand why the employee wants to follow this track. There may be other career options. Provide the employee with candid feedback, along with your own observations that support what it takes to be a successful leader and the current gap. However, this should not be the first time an employee receives the feedback.

Challenge 4: Similar to challenge 3, an employee wants to progress upward on a managerial track. Your assessment (based on behavioral examples) is that he does not have what it takes to be an effective manager at this time.

How to address: Ask, "Why do you want to be a manager?" or "Tell me more about why becoming a manager is important to you." By understanding why an employee wants a specific role, you will learn what motivates him. Sometimes employees assume that the only way to achieve a promotion and increased pay is to move into a managerial position. Career progression can also be realized by moving sideways or along an individual contributor track.

Challenge 5: You have a high-potential employee whom you want to promote. However, there are no available positions. You don't want to lose this key employee.

How to address: Use the aforementioned techniques to learn what will motivate and keep her engaged. Look at other options and help the employee develop in her current role.

Challenge 6: An employee raises concerns and frustrations about his current work. The conversation takes a turn toward focusing on these.

How to address: Acknowledge your employee's concerns, then guide him to find ways to move on with solutions. You might also find there are longstanding obstacles that you can address in your role as manager outside this meeting.

Challenge 7: An employee has indicated she will be retiring within the next two years and is not interested in a development plan.

How to address: Every employee's contribution is necessary and expected. Experienced employees have a wealth of skill and knowledge. For example, she could serve as a mentor or coach for her successor or for other employees who are less experienced or new to the company.

Challenge 8: Your employee is unfamiliar with the career and development planning process and has never before had a career discussion with his supervisor.

How to address: Spend additional time guiding your employee through the process. In this scenario it would be appropriate to do more telling than asking. In future cycles he will require a less directive approach.

Challenge 9: Your employee does production work and is not interested in additional advancement.

How to address: Employees may develop skills, knowledge, and competencies at any level. For example, an employee can learn to work more effectively in a team or learn more advanced skills for his current role. He can also learn new skills for other roles, thereby building in flexibility for your team if someone is out sick, leaves the company, or moves into another position. Job

rotations can facilitate this learning—but be sure to clarify this upon hiring. Macro-scale changes, such as implementation of a new enterprise system or an acquisition, may require the need for new skills, knowledge, and roles at many levels of the company.

Challenge 10: You and your employees are concerned that there will not be enough time for their development. As important as it is to develop your team, managers and employees are accountable for meeting the day-to-day bottom-line business demands.

How to address: Assure employees that learning new abilities will ultimately help them in their current and future roles in the company. First, regular check-ins with your employees about progress on their IDPs do not require hour-long meetings. Second, brief and informal updates can suffice in gauging if the employee's plan is progressing. Third, set aside designated times for employee development, so your team can work it into their schedules. A creative example was implemented by Australian SaaS company Atlassian, where employees have one day per quarter to work on whatever projects they don't normally have time for.

Be Creative

Learning and development opportunities are boundless. While identifying learning activities with your employees, encourage them (and yourself) to find creative options.

Example A: Learning presentation skills does not need to be limited to work options. Speaking at a church, at a Toastmasters meeting, and in low-risk situations will foster strength and confidence that will transfer to a work environment. Asking open-ended who, what, where, and how questions promotes new ideas: "How do you learn best? Where else could you practice presentations? Whom have you seen give outstanding presentations? What captured your attention?"

Example B: Managing projects is a valuable skill for any employee, particularly at the professional and manager levels. Projects can vary in size, although they usually incorporate common skill subsets such as organizing, influencing, prioritizing, planning, and communicating. Meaningful projects of any scope and complexity can serve as fertile ground for growth and measurable results. Specifically, for an associate level, organizing the logistics of a training program requires setting the target deadline, creating the plan, gaining input from others, listening, relating to others, organizing multiple resources, implementing, and measuring the outcome with feedback from stakeholders. In professional and managerial roles, projects and programs will require similar skills with higher stakes, visibility, challenges, and complexity.

Example C: Global leadership skill sets are a necessity for international companies. You cannot learn the competencies, knowledge, and skills required for success in a multicultural arena by only reading a book or watching videos. You'll accelerate learning and build confidence by doing, making mistakes, seeking feedback, building relationships, mentoring and coaching, and strengthening existing talents. Abilities learned through successful development plans at the managerial level become the foundation from which to launch new learning in the areas of visioning and strategy, global market competition, cultural norms, finances, leading change, leading multilayered divisions, profit and loss, growing a business, virtual leadership, and so on.

> WHILE IDENTIFYING LEARNING ACTIVITIES WITH YOUR EMPLOYEES, ENCOURAGE THEM (AND YOURSELF) TO FIND CREATIVE OPTIONS.

Formal programs and courses will continue to play a key role in learning and development. A 2015 Chartered Institute of Personnel and Development survey suggests a growing shift toward creating a learning culture, with increased use of internal knowledge-sharing events, job rotation, shadowing, action learning sets, and collaborative and social learning. A quarter of the respondents anticipate greater use of user-generated content, reflecting the need for agility and flexibility in meeting individual needs.

CONCLUSION

Generally, demonstrating your investment in your employees will go a long way toward motivating and retaining them, regardless of their unique circumstances. Employees want good supervision, coaching, and professional development. "Job seekers from entry-level to executive are more concerned with opportunities for learning and development than any other aspect of a prospective job," wrote Monique Valcour in a 2014 article in the *Harvard Business Review*. "This makes perfect sense, since continuous learning is a key strategy for crafting a sustainable career . . . Thus, employees' direct managers are often their most important developers."

As you create an actionable plan, periodically revisit the IDP process map to determine where you are. Once the plan is under way, your employees should be able to have open and trusting conversations with you about their careers and professional development. Take the time to listen, offer support, and encourage them to continue taking risks and learning.

Employee development is not a panacea for attracting and retaining good talent. However, it is a key competitive advantage in a complex and challenging business environment. You do not have to be a career counselor to be effective in your role in developing your employees, and it is satisfying to see an employee grow professionally with your support. By providing opportunity, guidance, and resources, you can realize the sweeping benefits that inspired employees bring to their role, their work, and their organization.

Books, Reports, and Education Programs

Association for Talent Development. 2015. ATD Integrated Talent Management Certificate Program. Alexandria, VA: ATD Press.

Butterfield, L., V. Lalande, and D. Borgen. 2009. *Career Conversations Literature Review*. Report number 5. Ottawa: Canadian Research Working Group. www.crwg-gdrc.ca/crwg/wp-content /uploads/2010/10/Report-5-CC-Literature -Review3.pdf.

Chartered Institute of Personnel and Development (CIPD). 2015. *Annual Survey Report: Learning and Development*. London: CIPD. www.cipd.co.uk /binaries/learning-development_2015.pdf.

Lombardo, M.M., and R.W. Eichinger. 2004. *FYI: For Your Improvement, a Guide for Development and Coaching*. 4th ed. Minneapolis: Lominger.

Shi, Y.D. 2012. *Career Development 2012 Benchmark Study*. Melbourne, Australia: Right Management.

Articles and Press Releases

Arash. 2014. "Manager Conversations That Keep Employees Happy." 7Geese blog, June 5. https://7geese.com/manager-conversations -that-keep-employees-happy.

Bureau of Labor Statistics. 2015. "Employment Situation Summary." Bureau of Labor Statistics, July 2. www.bls.gov/news.release/empsit.nr0 .htm.

Connolly, M. 2015. "The Kurt Lewin Change Management Model." Change Management Coach. www.change-management-coach.com /kurt_lewin.html.

EdAssist. 2015. "Millennials Desperate for Financial Stability, in Search of Employer Support to Get There." Yahoo! Finance, April 8. http://finance. yahoo.com/news/millennials-desperate- financial-stability-search-160600187.html.

Ginac, L. 2014. "Why Managers Need to Be Career Coaches." Career Development Blog, November 3. Alexandria, VA: ATD Press.

Hosmer, D. "Coaching With Questions." *Training Journal*, September 2015, forthcoming.

Kaiden, S. 2015. "Keeping Your Career on Track." *TD at Work*. Alexandria, VA: ATD Press.

Kaye, B., and J. Winkle Giulioni. 2012. "Career Development Conversations: Overcoming Common Myths." T+D 66(5): 30-31.

Olesen, C., D. White, and I. Lemmer. 2007. "Career Models and Culture Change at Microsoft." *Organizational Development Journal* 25(2): 31-35.

Raque, R. 2014. "Manager as Career Coach? Really?" Right Management, December 10. www.right .com/wps/wcm/connect/right-us-en/home /thoughtwire/categories/talent-work /manager-as-career-coach-really.

Relf, S. 2014. "Engage Millennial Workers With a Strong Development Scheme." *Training Journal*, October 24. www.trainingjournal.com/articles /feature/engage-millennial-workers-strong -development-scheme.

Schawbel, D. 2014. "10 Workplace Trends for 2015." *Forbes*, October 29. www.forbes.com /sites/danschawbel/2014/10/29/the-top-10 -workplace-trends-for-2015.

Valcour, M. 2014. "If You're Not Helping People Develop, You're Not Management Material." *Harvard Business Review*, January 23. https://hbr .org/2014/01/if-youre-not-helping-people -develop-youre-not-management-material.

Wacek, K. 2015. "Client Wins 2015 Training Magazine Best Practice Award." Career Systems International blog, February 17. http:// careersystemsintl.com/client-wins-2015 -training-magazine-best-practice-award.

Online Resources

aLife. www.alife.net.au

edX. www.edx.org

www.linkedin.com

Mind Tools. www.mindtools.com/pages/main
/newMN_CDV.htm

myfuture. www.myfuture.edu.au

O*NET OnLine. www.onetonline.org

CAREER AND DEVELOPMENT DISCUSSION PREPARATION WORKSHEET

Use this worksheet to help prepare for a career and development discussion with your manager.

Meeting Preparation

Questions	My Answers
What do I hope to accomplish from my development discussion with my manager?	
What is important to me personally (e.g., family, job location, salary, work-life balance)?	
What are my career aspirations? (complete table below)	
How does my current role fit in my career vision?	
What are my current skill, knowledge, and competency strengths?	
What must I develop to be more successful for my current role and my career?	
What new projects, assignments, or responsibilities could stretch my learning?	
What resources and support do I need to progress in my career path?	
Who could support my development?	
What questions do I have for my manager?	
Have I scheduled an initial career or IDP meeting with my manager?	

Career Aspirations

Short-Term Career Objective (0-2 years):	
Long-Term Career Vision (3-5 years):	

MY CAREER AND INDIVIDUAL DEVELOPMENT PLAN

Name: _____ Manager: _____

Date: _____

Career Aspirations

Short-Term Career Objective (0-2 years):	
Long-Term Career Vision (3-5 years):	

Development Plan

Learning Objective	Activity	Resources	Completion Date	Success Measure
What will I know or be able to do as a result of the activity?	How will I meet the objective?	Who or what will be necessary to accomplish the objective?	When will I have met the learning objective?	How will I know I have accomplished the objective?

First check-in meeting date: _____